A FUN GUIDE TO BASEBALL!

THIS BOOK BELONGS TO

PLAYFUL PLANET
KIDS SHOW

AI Disclaimer

This book was created with the help of advanced AI tools, including Adobe Firefly and ChatGPT, to generate and refine content and imagery. While these technologies were instrumental in providing initial drafts and ideas, every element in this book has been heavily edited, curated, and customized to ensure accuracy, creativity, and alignment with the vision of the Playful Planet universe.

The original characters and their stories remain wholly unique and are the result of the author's creative process. The AI tools were used to enhance efficiency and provide inspiration, but the final product is a reflection of human creativity, passion, and dedication.

Thank you for supporting transparency and creativity in this evolving digital age.

Copyright

Disclaimer: Accuracy of Information

The information provided in this book is based on well-researched facts about soccer. We have made every effort to ensure the accuracy of the information presented; however, please note that the rules, terminology, and understanding of soccer may evolve over time. The information in this book is accurate as of the year of publication.

This book is designed to entertain and educate young readers about soccer in a fun and engaging way. It is not intended to serve as a complete official rulebook or coaching manual, but rather as an introduction to the exciting and fast-paced world of soccer.

Introduction

Baseball is more than just a game—it's a tradition that brings people together and creates lifelong memories. For over a century, kids and adults have stepped onto the diamond, swung for the fences, and cheered on their favorite teams with excitement and pride. From neighborhood sandlots to professional stadiums packed with fans, baseball is a sport that encourages teamwork, patience, strategy, and determination.

Whether you're tossing a ball in the backyard, practicing with your school team, or dreaming of playing in the World Series someday, baseball offers something for everyone. It's a game of skill and smarts, where every pitch, hit, and catch can change the outcome in a heartbeat.

In this book, you'll learn:

- The rules of the game and how to play it the right way

- Where you can play baseball and how to start, even with just a ball and a glove

- What equipment you'll need to play safely and confidently

- Step-by-step breakdowns of important skills and strategies like pitching, hitting, and base running

- Profiles of some of the most legendary baseball players who made history and inspired millions

- Fun activities, stat trackers, and glossary pages to help you remember everything you learn

Whether you're just starting out or already swinging for the fences, this guide is your all-in-one playbook to understanding and loving the game of baseball. So grab your glove, lace up your cleats, and let's get ready to play

Chapter 1:

The Basics of Baseball

Baseball is a team sport played between two teams of nine players each. The goal is to score more runs than the other team by hitting the ball and running around four bases in a diamond shape.

- **Four bases** – home plate, first base, second base, third base

- **Pitcher's mound** – where the pitcher stands

- **Infield** – area around the bases

- **Outfield** – grassy area beyond the bases

- **Dugouts** – where players sit when not on the field

A baseball field has:

Chapter 2:

How to Play

Baseball is played in innings, usually nine, where each team gets a turn to bat and a turn to field.

1. **Pitching** – The pitcher throws the ball toward the batter.

2. **Batting** – The batter tries to hit the ball and run to first base.

3. **Running**– The player runs around the bases to score a run.

4. **Fielding** - The fielding team tries to get the batter or runners out.

Each team tries to score runs by hitting the ball and running

Here's how it works:

Chapter 3:

The Rules of the Game

To play fair and have fun, here are some important rules to remember:

What refs wear!

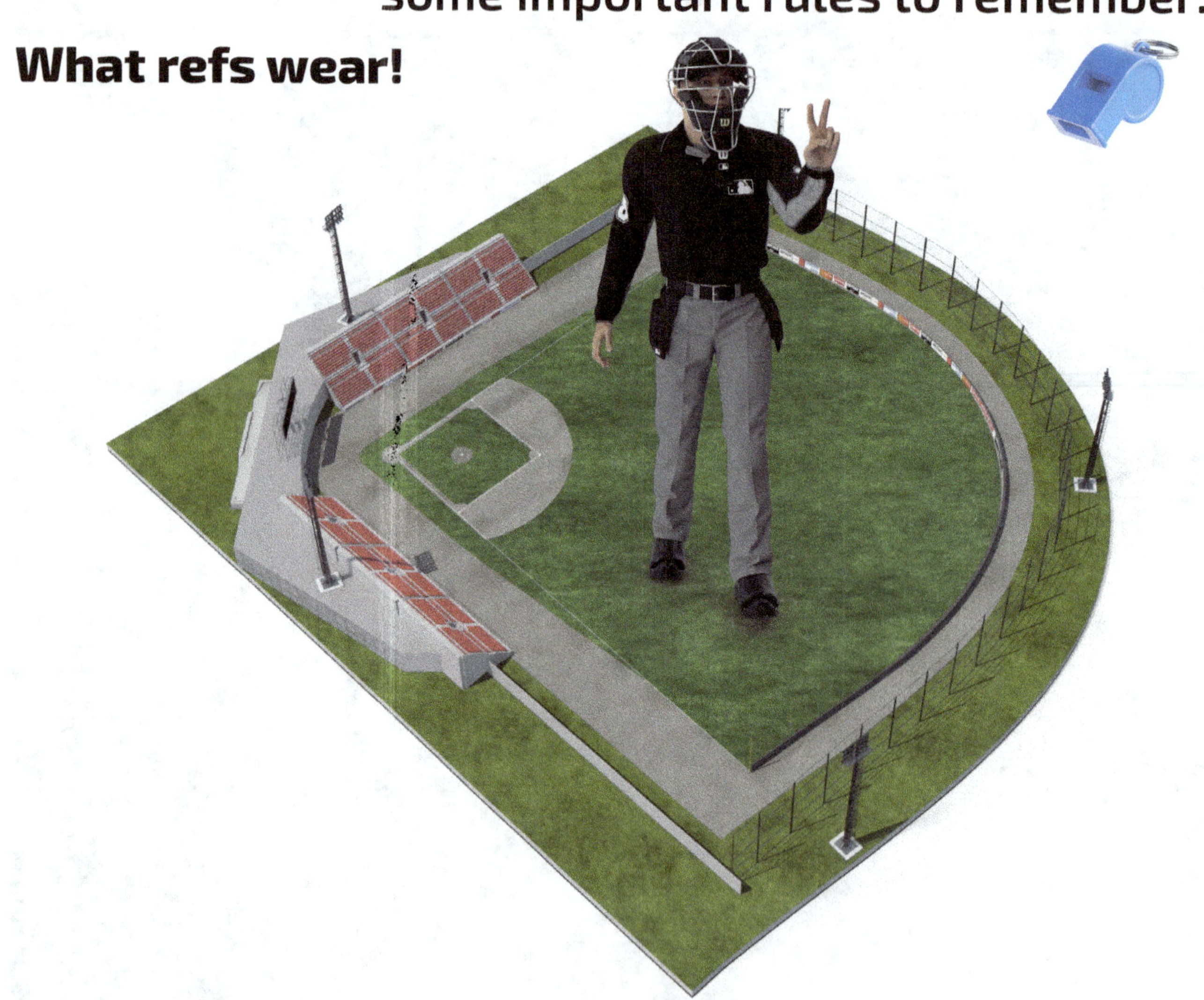

- Each team has nine players on the field.

- A batter gets three strikes before they're out.

- If a batter gets four balls, they walk to first base.

- A team gets three outs, then the other team bats.

- A run is scored when a player touches all four bases.

- A foul ball is when the ball is hit outside the lines of play.

- A home run is when the ball is hit out of the park and the batter runs all the bases!

important rules to follow:

Chapter 4:

Where to Play
You can play baseball in all kinds of places:

- Baseball fields in parks or schools

- Backyards (with soft balls or plastic bats)

- T-ball fields for younger players

- Recreation centers and little league teams

If you don't have a full field, you can play simple games like catch, home run derby, or whiffle ball.

A Baseball field:

Chapter 5:

What You Need to Play
Here's what you need to get started:

- Baseball glove to catch the ball

- Bat (choose the right size for your age)

- Baseball (or a soft ball for younger kids)

- Batting helmet to protect your head

- Baseball cleats or sneakers

- Comfortable clothes or uniform

- Water bottle to stay hydrated

A baseball game:

Team

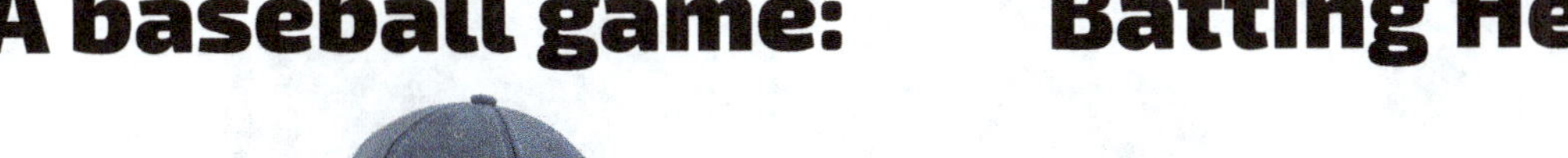

Batting Helmet

Water Bottle

Baseball Cap

Cleats

Uniform

Baseball

Chapter 6:

Basic Strategies and Cool Moves

To play smarter and have more fun, try these strategies and moves: Practice these and you'll be a smart player in no time!

Basic Strategies:

- **Hit and run** – The runner starts running as soon as the batter swings.

- **Double play** – Two outs made in one play.

- **Tagging up**– Wait on the base before running after a fly ball is caught.

Cool Moves:

- **Sliding into a base**– Helps avoid being tagged out.

- **Catching a fly ball** – Important for defense.

- **Throwing to the cutoff** – Helps get the ball back in quickly.

- **Bunting**– A soft hit to surprise the defense.

Basic Strategies:

Chapter 7:

Famous Baseball Players

Here are some legendary players who made baseball history:

- **Babe Ruth**– One of the greatest home run hitters ever.

- **Jackie Robinson**– Broke the color barrier and inspired millions.

- **Derek Jeter** – Known for clutch plays and leadership.

- **Shohei Ohtani** – A modern superstar who pitches and hits.

- **Mookie Betts**–A speedy outfielder with a powerful bat.

- **Roberto Clemente** – An amazing player and humanitarian.

LEGENDS

Chapter 8: Baseball sizes

9–9.25 inches

9 inches

9 inches

Type	Circumference	Weight	Recommended Age	Common Use
T-ball Baseball	9 inches	4.5 oz (lighter)	Ages 4–7	Youth leagues, casual play
Youth Baseball	9 inches	5–5.25 oz	Ages 8–12	Youth leagues
Official Baseball	9–9.25 inches	5–5.25 oz	Ages 13+ (High School+)	High school, college
Material:	Leather or synthetic cover with raised seams	**Core:**	Cork and rubber center wound with yarn	

Baseball Bat Sizes

11–13 years 28–31 inches

Weight Drop (Length - Weight)
-8 to -10

8–10 years 26–29 inches

Weight Drop (Length - Weight)
-10 to -12

5–7 years 24–26 inches

Weight Drop (Length - Weight)
-10 to -13

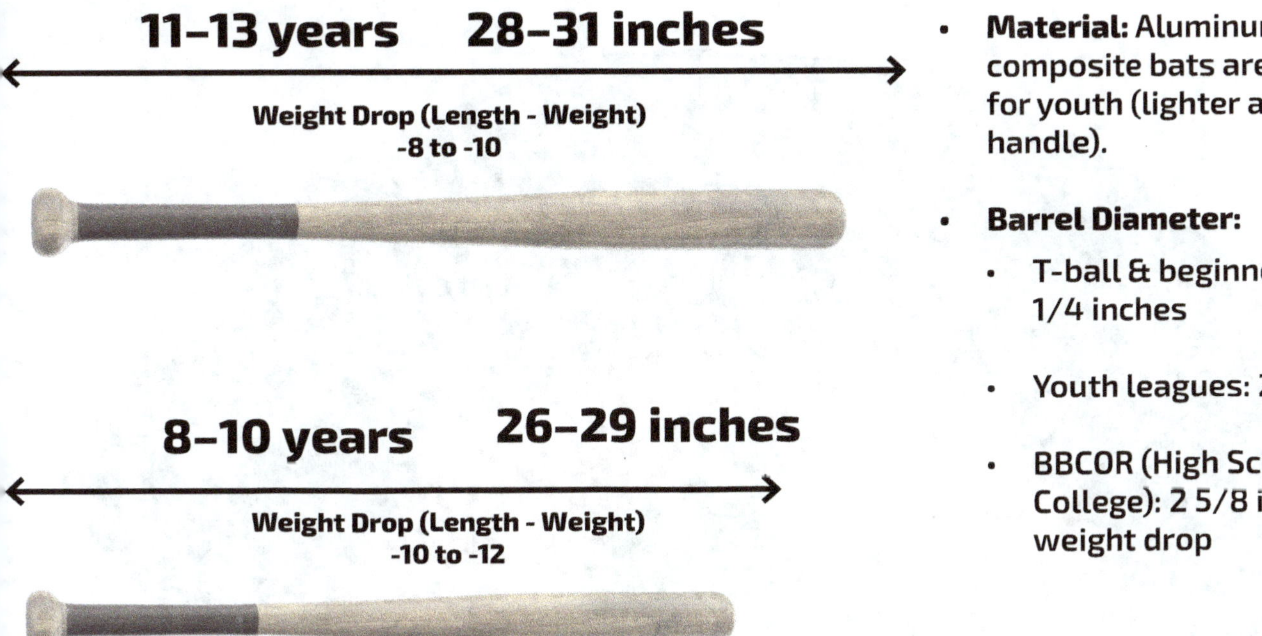

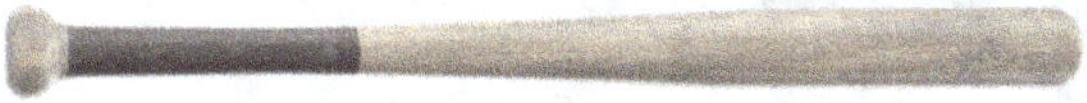

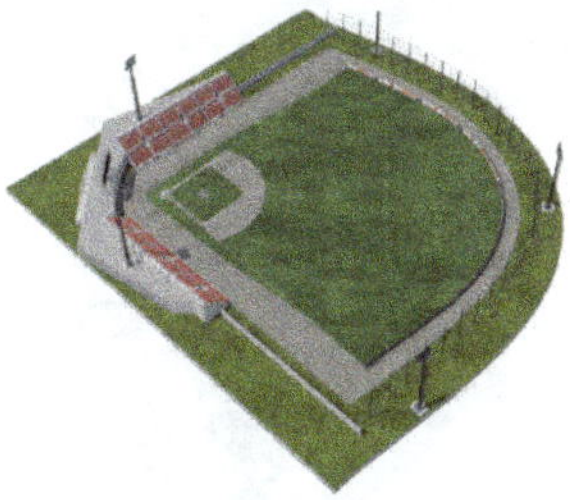

- **Material:** Aluminum or composite bats are common for youth (lighter and easier to handle).
- **Barrel Diameter:**
  - T-ball & beginner bats: 2 1/4 inches
  - Youth leagues: 2 5/8 inches
  - BBCOR (High School/ College): 2 5/8 inches, -3 weight drop

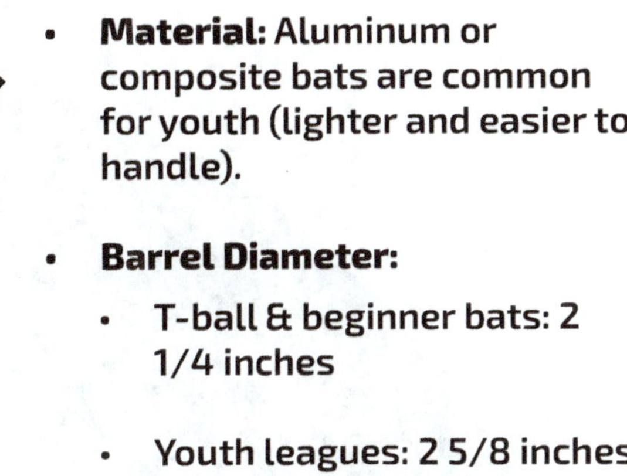

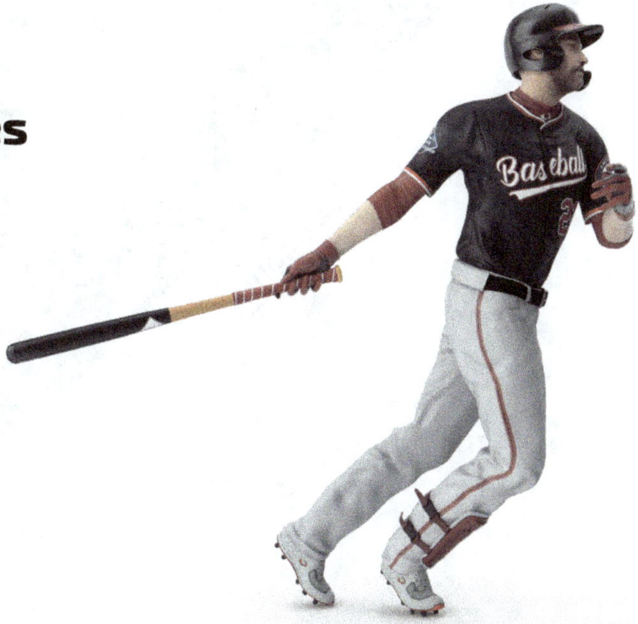

Baseball field Specs

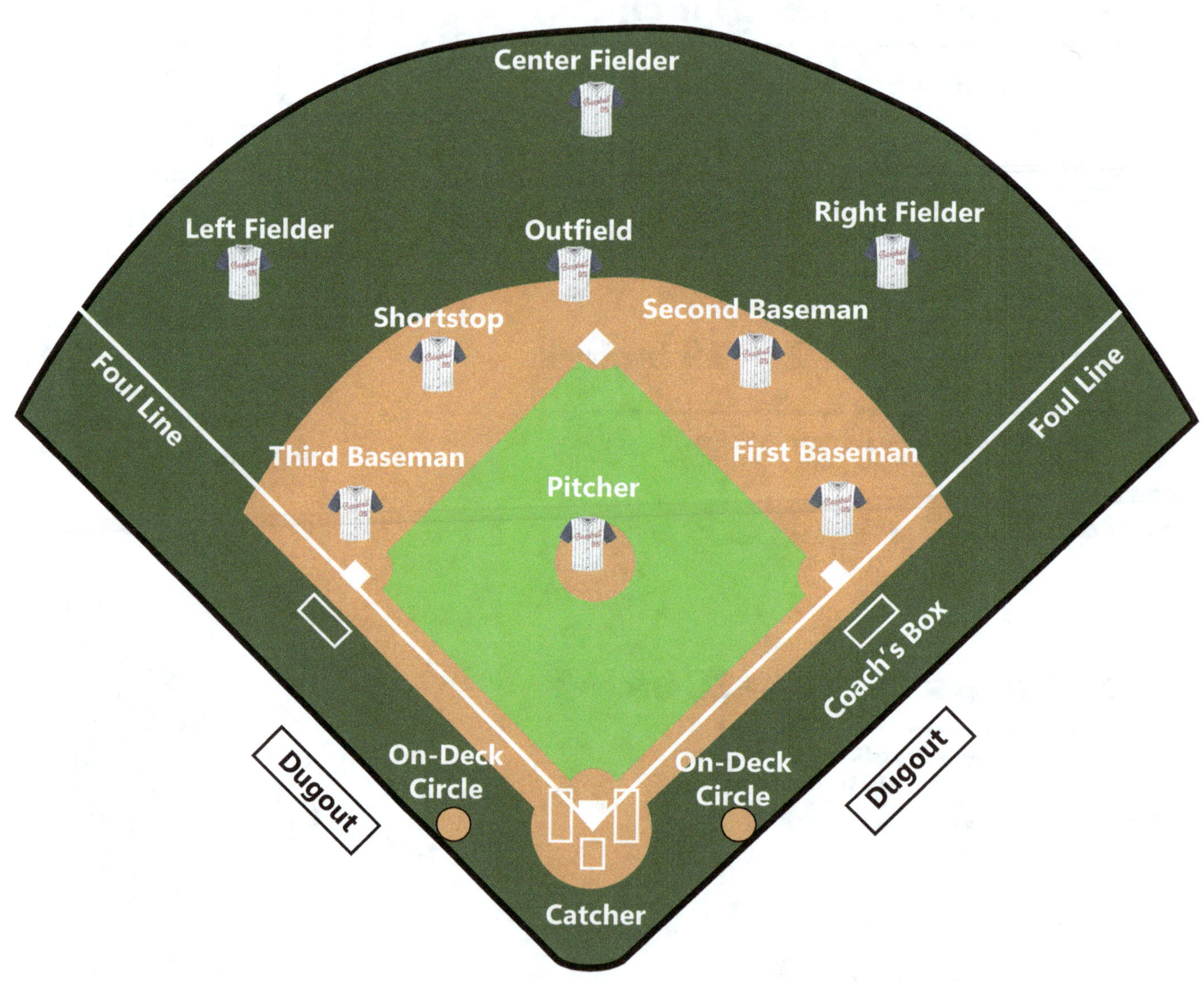

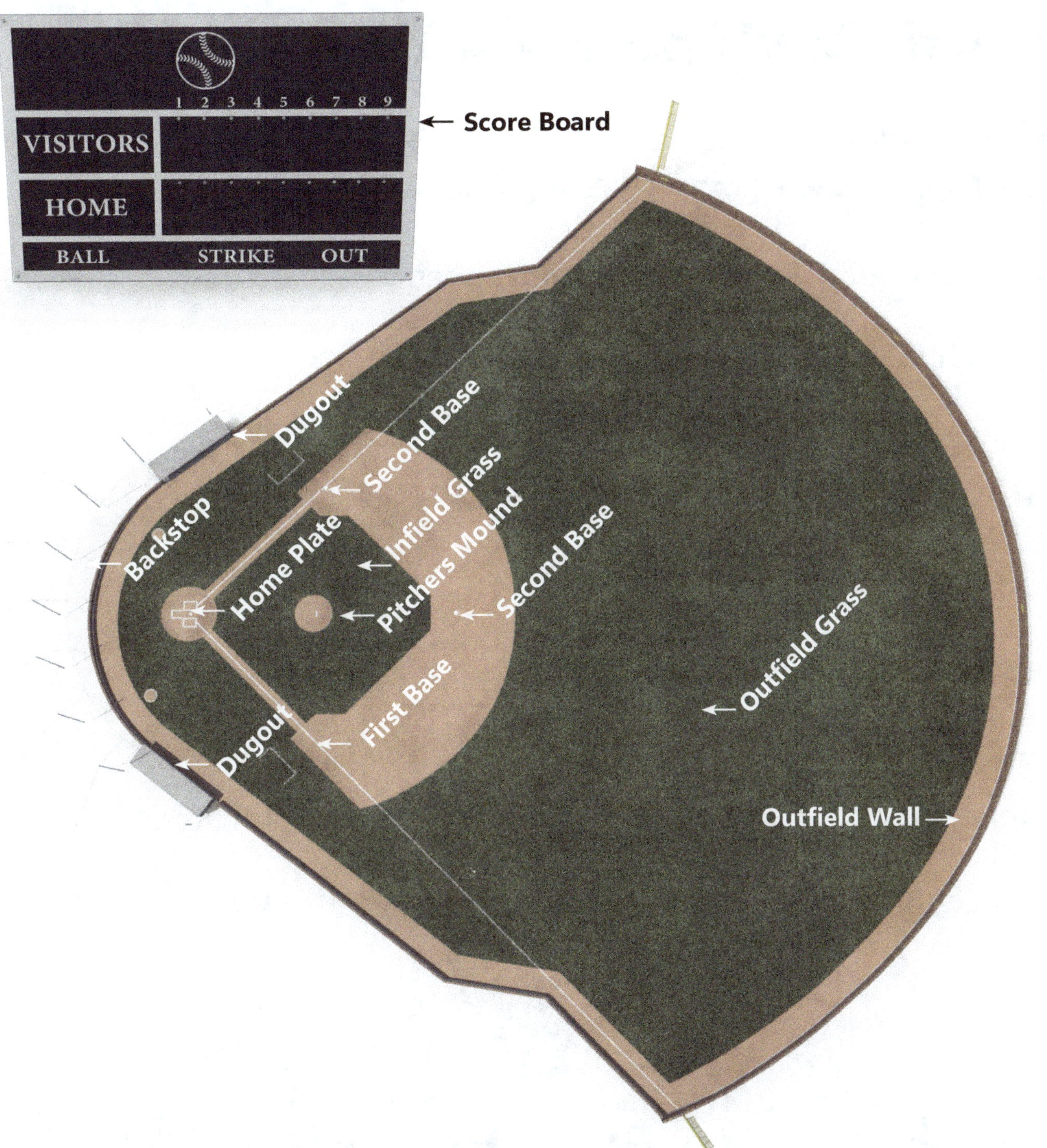
Score Board
1 2 3 4 5 6 7 8 9
VISITORS
HOME
BALL   STRIKE   OUT
Dugout
Second Base
Infield Grass
Backstop
Home Plate
Pitchers Mound
Second Base
Outfield Grass
First Base
Dugout
Outfield Wall

Baseball Field Specs and Dimensions

Base Path Lengths

- Little League (Ages 9–12): 60 feet between bases

- Middle School: 70–80 feet between bases

- High School & MLB: 90 feet between bases

Pitcher's Mound to Home Plate

- Little League: 46 feet

- Middle School: 50–54 feet

- High School & MLB: 60 feet 6 inches

Infield

- Square-shaped "diamond" where all the bases are located

- Bases: First, Second, Third, and Home Plate form a perfect square

Baseball Field Specs and Dimensions

Outfield

- Grassy area beyond the bases

- Distance to Outfield Fence (approximate):

- Little League: 200 feet

- High School: 300–375 feet

- MLB: 325–400 feet depending on the stadium

Bases and Mound

- Bases: 15 inches × 15 inches

- Home Plate: Five-sided rubber plate, 17 inches wide

- Pitcher's Mound Height: 6–10 inches above home plate (10 inches in MLB)

- Pitcher's Plate (Rubber): 24 inches long

Baseball Fun Zone – Activities and Games!

Why Are Stats Important?

- They help you see your progress
- They show what you're good at and what you can work on
- They're fun to collect—like a personal scoreboard!

Match the Term! -Match the baseball term to what it means:

Stat	What It Means
Home Run	_____A. Three good pitches missed by the batter
Pitcher	_____ B. The person who throws the ball
Strikeout	_____ C. Hitting the ball out of the park
Inning	_____ D. A part of the game where both teams bat
Tag Out	_____ E. Touching a runner with the ball to get them out

Challenge Questions!

1. Which stat do pitchers care about the most?
   a) Hits
   b) Strikeouts
   c) Runs
2. If you got 2 hits and scored 1 run, how many times did you help your team?
   a) 1 time
   b) 2 times
   c) 3 times
3. Which stat shows how well you help your teammates score?
   a) RBIs (Runs Batted In)
   b) Strikeouts
   c) Catches

Activity: Track Your Game Stats!

Instructions: Keep score like the pros! Fill in your stats after a practice or game.

Game #	Hits	Runs	At Bats	Strikeouts	Catches	Throws
1						
2						
3						
4						
5						
6						

Bonus: Star your best game!

Baseball Quiz Time!

Instructions: Test your baseball

1. How many players are on a baseball team during a game?
   a) 7   b) 9   c) 11

2. What's it called when the batter hits the ball out of the park?
   a) Pop fly   b) Home run   c) Strike

3. What do you wear on your hand to catch the ball?
   a) Helmet   b) Bat   c) Glove

4. What's a "double play"?
   a) Two players run at once
   b) Two outs in one play
   c) Two hits in a row

Baseball Hall of Fame Scrapbook

Cut out pictures of your favorite players or teams and glue them here. Or draw them yourself!

Who is your favorite baseball player and why?

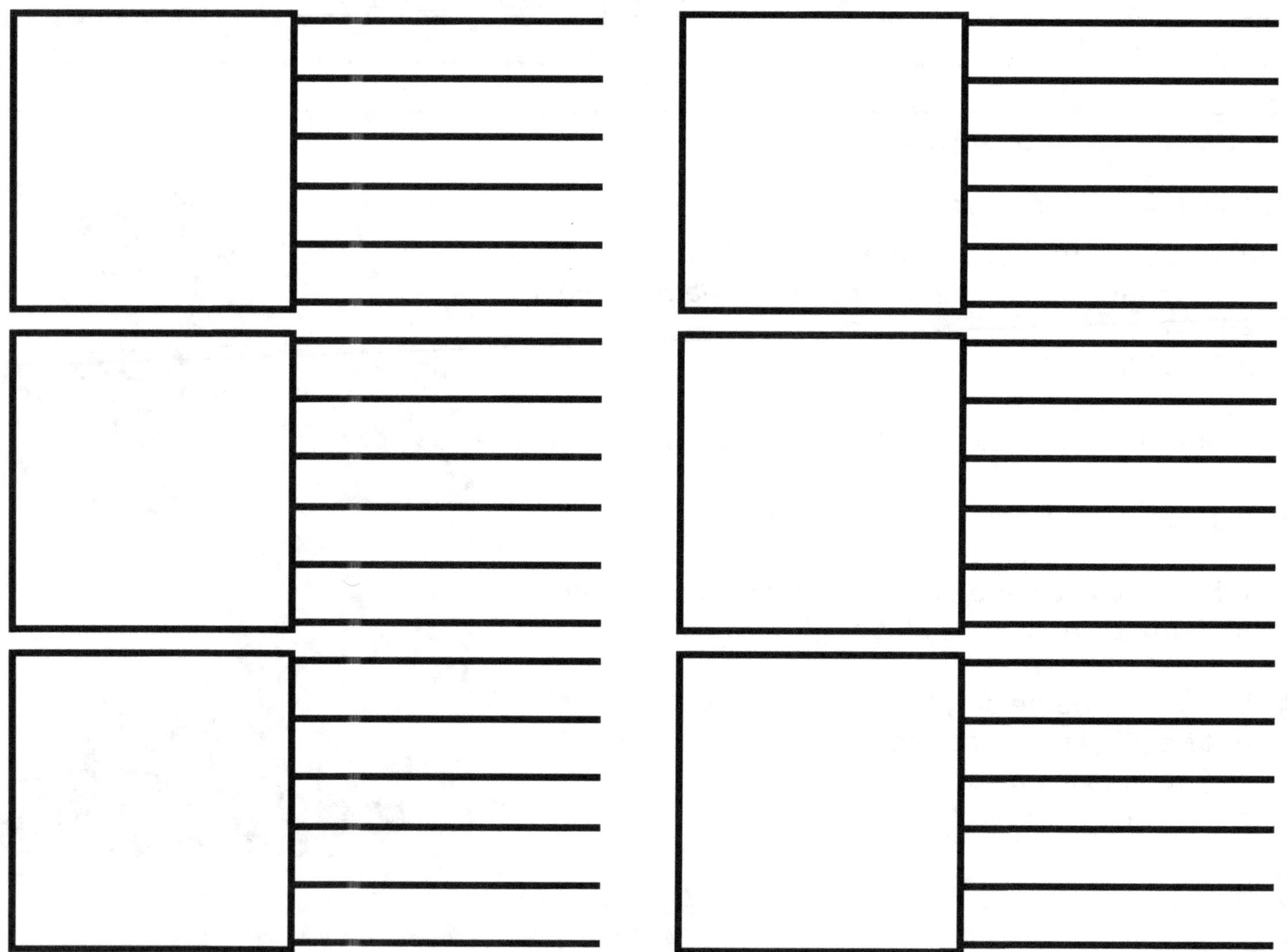

Baseball Scavenger Hunt

Instructions: Can you spot all these during a game or practice? Check them off!

- ☐ Someone sliding into a base
- ☐ A home run
- ☐ A double play
- ☐ A glove catch
- ☐ A team huddle
- ☐ A scoreboard
- ☐ A batter wearing helmet and cleats
- ☐ A coach giving signals

Label the Field (Visual Activity)

Instructions: Can you draw and label the parts of a baseball field?

Draw lines to connect the names to the correct spot on the field:

- Home Plate

- First Base

- Second Base

- Third Base

- Pitcher's Mound

- Infield

- Outfield

- Dugout

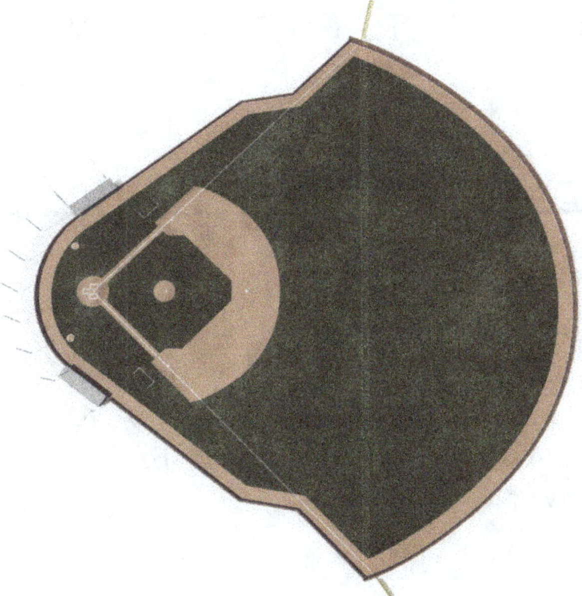

Baseball Word Search

N	S	J	C	E	X	Z	P	O	B	A	S	E	U	X	N	V	X
M	K	T	T	M	V	G	P	H	K	J	K	G	R	X	C	B	T
U	E	D	R	X	Z	Z	H	O	M	E	R	U	N	E	Z	P	S
R	O	M	K	I	W	T	V	T	S	J	S	F	K	K	T	T	R
C	M	Q	C	R	K	M	C	K	E	H	W	M	L	X	K	E	B
L	P	I	T	C	H	E	R	T	C	R	I	W	F	P	P	A	Z
J	G	I	O	U	T	F	I	E	L	D	N	D	Y	U	G	M	C
E	L	J	N	W	I	K	L	Q	B	M	G	Z	U	O	L	F	G
G	X	U	V	M	F	H	S	F	J	A	G	R	G	Q	O	M	V
Y	E	S	O	W	S	L	Q	T	S	G	T	Q	V	E	V	G	F
L	M	K	S	P	U	Z	S	Z	C	A	T	C	H	M	E	M	R
Y	O	B	G	W	K	A	J	P	N	G	F	P	B	V	A	E	Y

Find the following words in the puzzle.
Words are hidden →, ↓, and ↘.

OUTFIELD	GLOVE	TEAM
PITCHER	CATCH	BAT
HOME RUN	SWING	
STRIKE	BASE	

Key Baseball Stats for Kids

Baseball stats are short for statistics. They are numbers used to track how well a player performs during games. Coaches, players, and even fans use stats to understand how a player helps their team. It's like a scoreboard for your skills!

Here are some basic baseball stats kids can track:

- Hits (H): How many times you hit the ball and get on base

- Runs (R): How many times you run all the way around the bases and score

- At Bats (AB): How many times you come up to hit

- Strikeouts (SO or K): How many times you strike out

- Catches (C): How many fly balls or line drives you catch

- Throws (T): How many good throws you make to teammates

- RBIs (Runs Batted In): How many teammates score because of your hit

- Walks (BB): How many times you get to first base from four balls (a "base on balls")

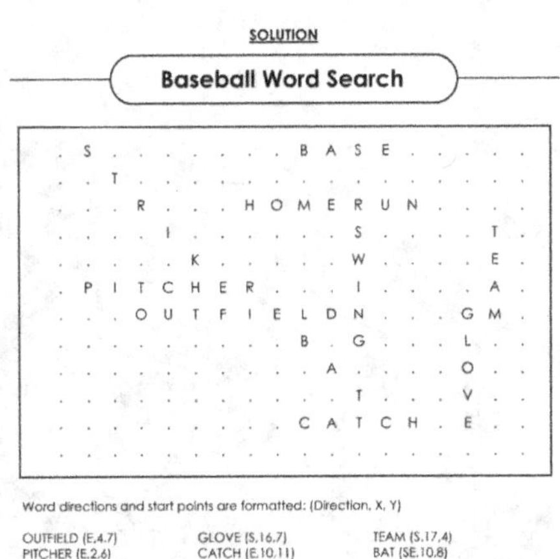

Conclusion

Baseball is an amazing sport that teaches teamwork, focus, and fun. Whether you're playing in a league or just throwing the ball with a friend, baseball is a great way to enjoy the outdoors and challenge yourself. Now that you know the rules, skills, and cool moves—grab your glove and step up to the plate!

- **Strike** – A pitch the batter misses or doesn't swing at in the strike zone.

- **Home run** – Hitting the ball out of the park and scoring a run.

- **Pitcher** – The player who throws the ball to the batter.

- **Out** – When a player is removed from the field after three strikes, a tag, or a catch.

- **Base hit** – A hit that lets the batter safely reach a base.

- **Tag out** – Touching a runner with the ball while they're not on a base.

Happy playing!

Glossary

Athletics

Design Your Own Baseball Jersey

Instructions:

Draw and color your dream baseball jersey. Don't forget your team name, number, and favorite colors!

Think About:

What animal or symbol could represent your team?
What colors make your team stand out?

Design Your Own Baseball Jersey

Design Your Own Baseball Jersey

Design Your Own Baseball Jersey

Color Me

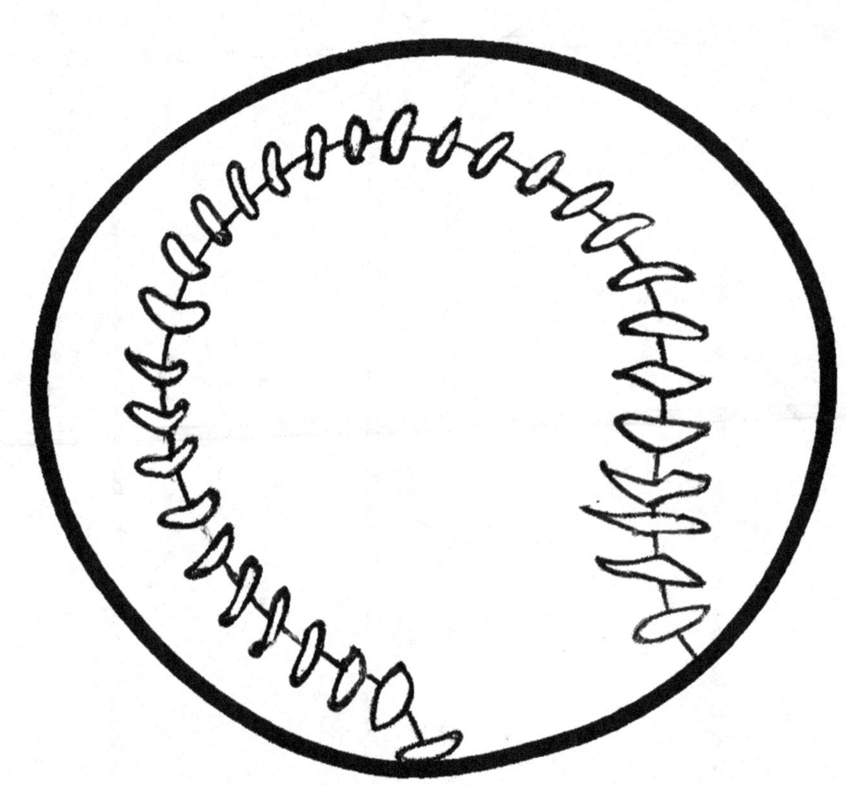

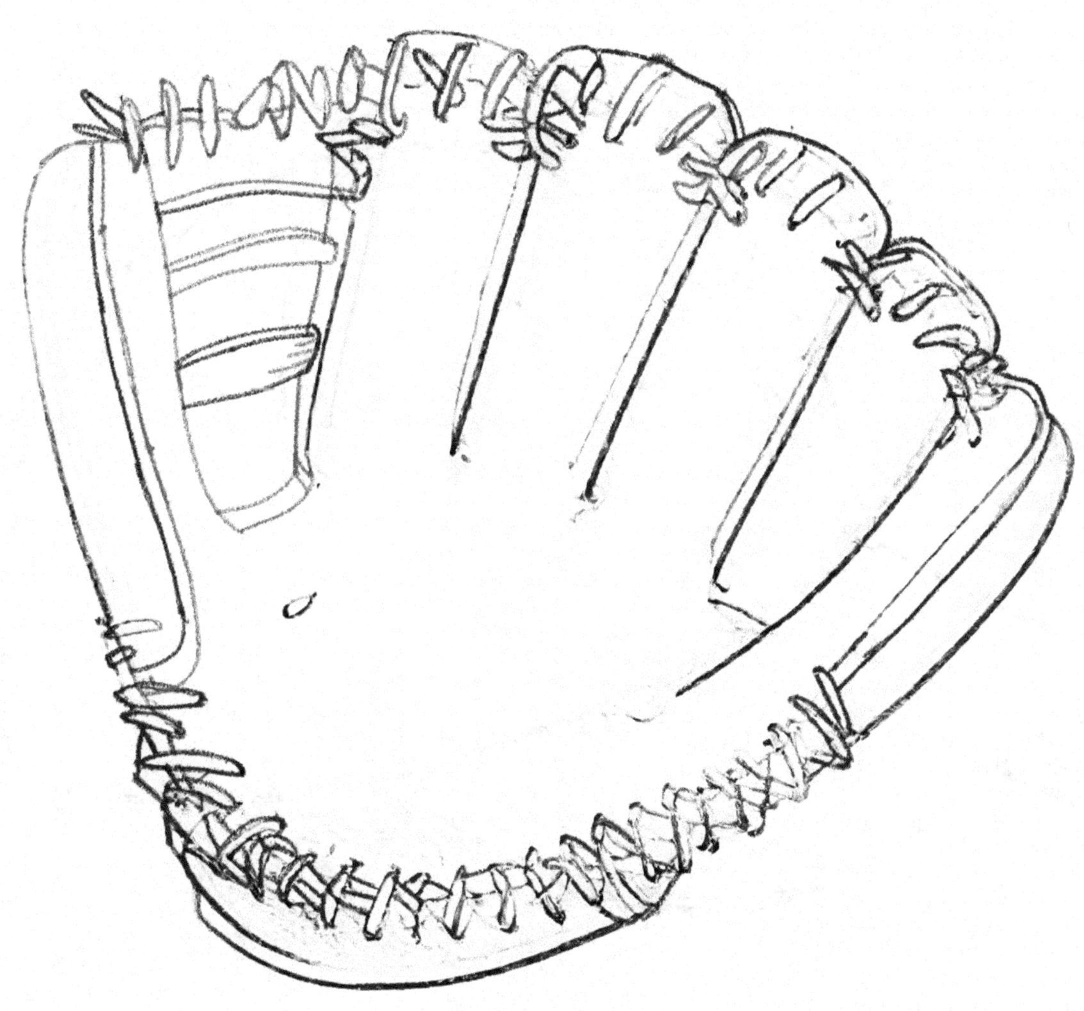

Color Me

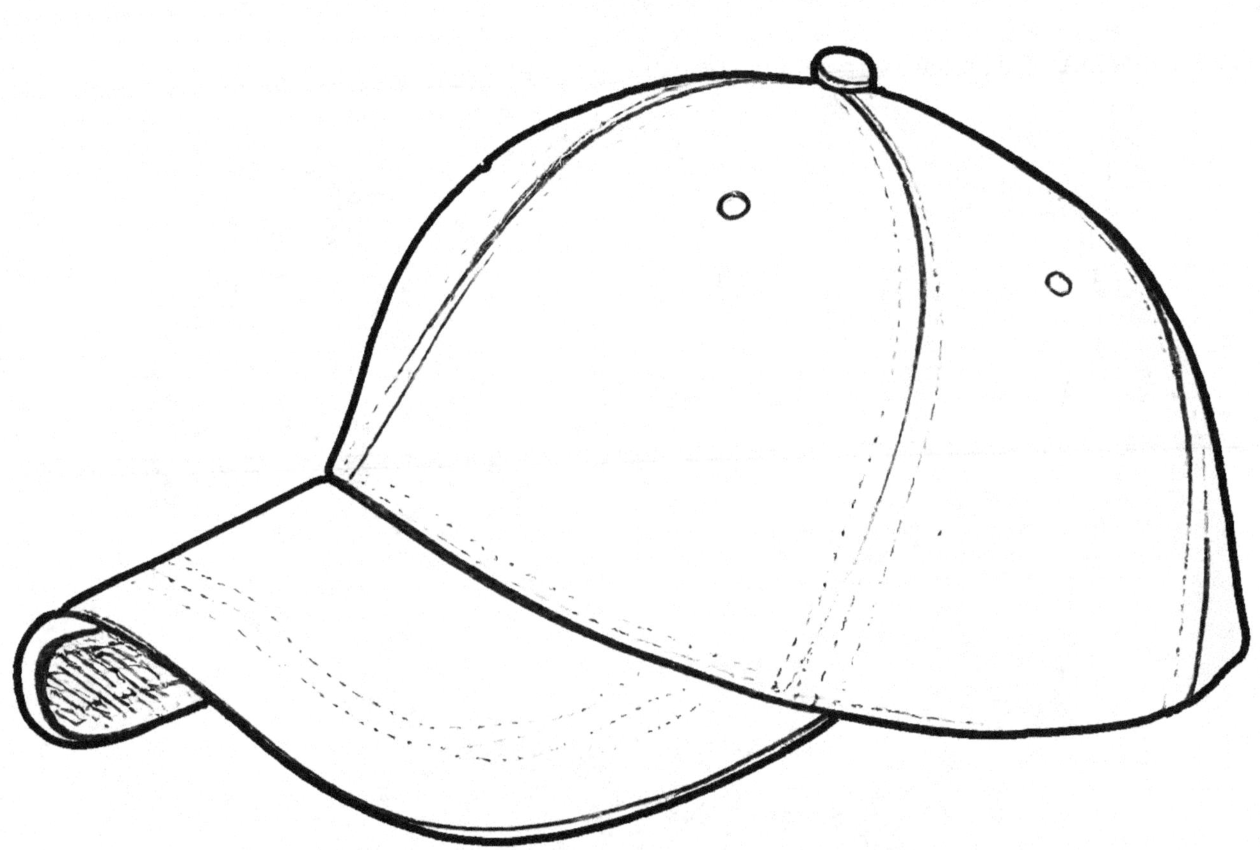

Color Me

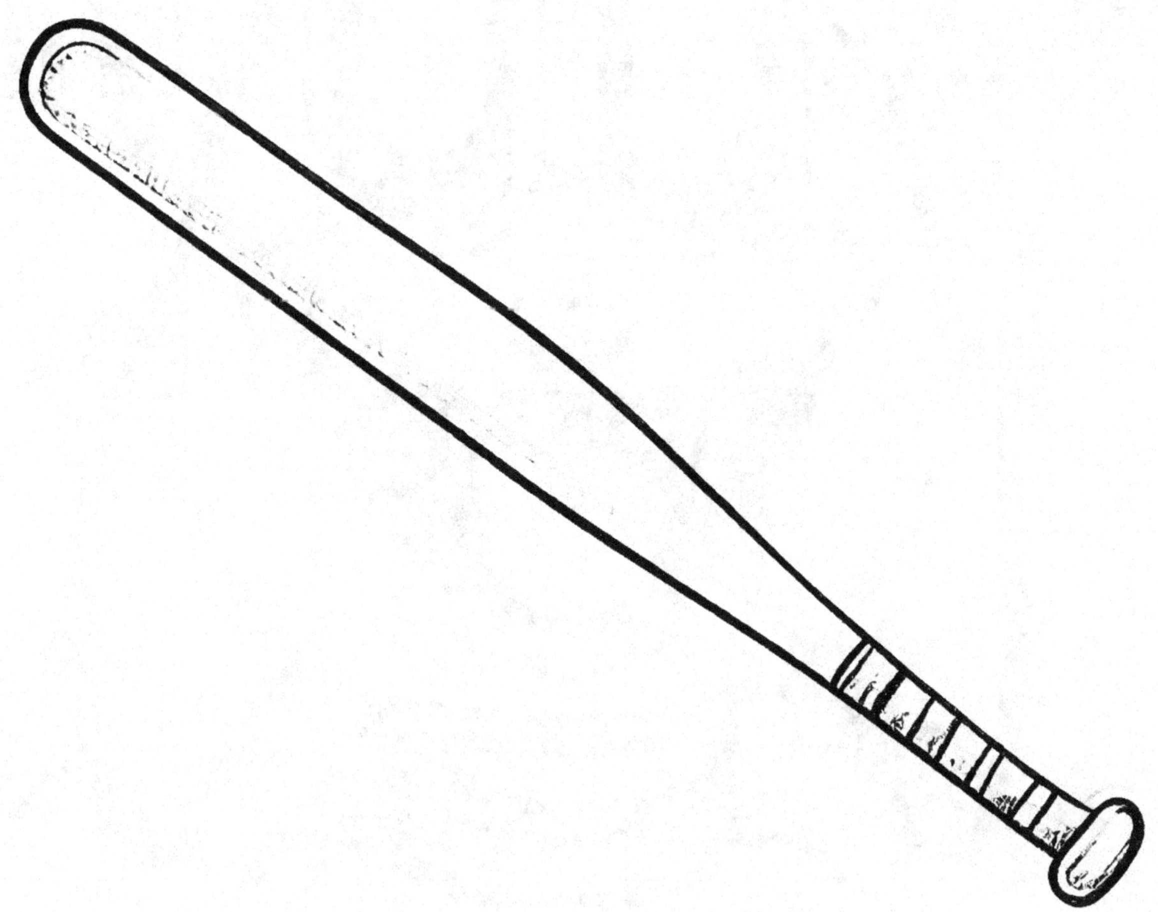

AMAZON STORE
YOUTUBE SUBSCRIBE
PLAYFUL PLANET KIDS SHOW
ROCK-IT

AMAZON STORE
PLAYFUL PLANET KIDS SHOW
PIPPY
YOUTUBE SUBSCRIBE

AMAZON STORE
YOUTUBE SUBSCRIBE
PLAYFUL PLANET KIDS SHOW
STARSHINE

AMAZON STORE
PLAYFUL PLANET KIDS SHOW
YOUTUBE
SUBSCRIBE
ASTROID

AMAZON STORE
YOUTUBE
SUBSCRIBE
PLAYFUL PLANET KIDS SHOW
SUNNY

PLAYFACE
PLANET
KIDS SHOW
AMAZON
STORE
YOUTUBE
SUBSCRIBE
LUNAR

PLAYFUL
PLANET
KIDS SHOW
AMAZON
STORE
YOUTUBE
SUBSCRIBE

THIS CERTIFICATE IS PRESENTED

GREAT JOB!

DATE

PARENT NOTES

Parents and caregivers are invited to watch alongside their little ones. We encourage you to actively participate, imitate sounds, and engage in the activities shown on the screen to enhance your child's learning and development.

Welcome to **[Preschool with Pippy]**, where the magic of reading and writing begins!
At **age 3**, your child is embarking on an exciting journey of literacy development. By now, they should be showing signs of readiness for reading and writing, including:

- **Language Skills:** Your child may be using more complex sentences and expanding their vocabulary daily. They may also enjoy rhymes, songs, and storytelling.

- **Print Awareness:** Look for signs that your child recognizes letters and numbers in their environment, such as on signs, labels, and books. They may also be interested in scribbling and drawing, demonstrating an early understanding of writing.

- **Interest in Books:** Encourage your child's love for books by reading together regularly. They may enjoy simple stories with colorful illustrations and may even begin to "read" familiar books by memory.

- **Fine Motor Skills:** Developing fine motor skills is crucial for writing readiness. Activities such as drawing, coloring, and tracing lines can help strengthen these skills.

- **Curiosity and Engagement:** Your child's curiosity about the world around them is blossoming. Encourage their natural curiosity by providing opportunities for exploration and hands-on learning experiences.

As you read and explore The preschool with Pippy Series together, remember to celebrate your child's progress and enjoy this special time of growth and discovery.

Happy reading!

Playful Planet Kids Show.

www.ingramcontent.com/pod-product-compliance
Lightning Source LLC
Chambersburg PA
CBHW081229130726
47997CB00009B/2822